Dear Parent:
Your child's love of rea~~~

Every child learns to read in a differen[t] ~~~ [s]peed.
You can help your young reader impro~~~ [me]nt
by encouraging his or her own interest~ ~~~ [abilities]. You can also guide
your child's spiritual development by reading stories with biblical values
and Bible stories, like I Can Read! books published by Zonderkidz. From
books your child reads with you to the first books he or she reads alone,
there are I Can Read! books for every stage of reading:

SHARED READING
Basic language, word repetition, and whimsical
illustrations, ideal for sharing with your emergent reader.

BEGINNING READING
Short sentences, familiar words, and simple concepts for
children eager to read on their own.

READING WITH HELP
Engaging stories, longer sentences, and language play
for developing readers.

READING ALONE
Complex plots, challenging vocabulary, and high-interest
topics for the independent reader.

ADVANCED READING
Short paragraphs, chapters, and exciting themes for the
perfect bridge to chapter books.

I Can Read! books have introduced children to the joy of reading since
1957. Featuring award-winning authors and illustrators and a fabulous
cast of beloved characters, I Can Read! books set the standard for
beginning readers.

A lifetime of discovery begins with the magical words **"I Can Read!"**

Visit www.icanread.com for information on enriching your child's reading experience.
Visit www.zonderkidz.com for more Zonderkidz I Can Read! titles.

Anyone who believes in me will live,
even if he dies.

John 11 : 25

ZONDERKIDZ

Jesus Raises Lazarus
Copyright © 2011 by Zonderkidz
Illustrations © 2011 by Valerie Sokolova

Requests for information should be addressed to:
Zonderkidz, *Grand Rapids, Michigan 49530*

Library of Congress Cataloging-in-Publication Data

Bowman, Crystal.
    Jesus raises Lazarus / by Crystal Bowman.
        p. cm. — (I can read level. Level one)
    Illustrated by Valerie Sokolova.
    ISBN 978-0-310-72158-1 (softcover)
    1. Raising of Lazarus (Miracle)—Juvenile literature. I. Sokolova, Valerie. II. Title.
BT367.R36B68 2011
226.7'09505—dc22
[E]—dc
                                                 2010016484

Editor: *Mary Hassinger*
Art direction: *Jody Langley*

Printed in China

17 18 19 /SCC/ 10 9 8 7 6 5 4

Jesus Raises Lazarus

story by Crystal Bowman
pictures by Valerie Sokolova

A man named Lazarus was sick.

He lived in Bethany

with his two sisters.

Their names were Mary and Martha.

They were all friends of Jesus.

Mary and Martha wanted Jesus
to make their brother better.
They sent someone to tell Jesus
that Lazarus was sick.

When Jesus heard

that Lazarus was sick,

he did not go to see him right away.

Jesus waited for two whole days.

Then he said to his helpers,

"Let's go to Bethany

to see Lazarus."

Jesus' helpers did not want to go.
"The people will try to hurt you,"
they said to Jesus.

But Jesus said to his helpers,

"If we go while it is light,

we will be safe."

"Our friend Lazarus is just sleeping.
I will wake him up," said Jesus.
Jesus' helpers hoped that Lazarus
was having a good night's sleep.
"He must be getting better,"
they said.

But Jesus knew

that Lazarus had died.

When Jesus got to Bethany
the people were sad.
"Lazarus has been in his grave
for four days," they told Jesus.

Martha ran to meet Jesus.

"If you had been here," she said,

"my brother would not have died."

Jesus said to Martha,

"Your brother will be alive again.

Everyone who believes in me

will live forever.

Do you believe this, Martha?"

"Yes," said Martha.

"I know you are the Son of God."

Mary was very sad.

Martha went to her sister.

"Jesus is here," Martha said.

"He wants to see you."

So Mary went to see Jesus.

"If you had been here," she said,

"my brother would not have died."

Jesus was sad when he saw

Mary and Martha crying.

"Where is he?" asked Jesus.

"In his grave," they said.

"We will show you where it is."

Jesus went to the grave

where they had put Lazarus.

It was a cave with a big stone

in front of it.

"Move the stone away," said Jesus.

"It will be smelly," said Martha.

"He has been dead for four days."

"You will see God's glory
if you believe," said Jesus.
So they moved the big stone
away from the cave.

Jesus looked up to heaven.

He said to God,

"Thank you for hearing me.

You always hear me.

But I am praying out loud

so the people will believe

that you sent me."

Then Jesus said in a loud voice,

"Lazarus, come out!"

And Lazarus came out of the grave!

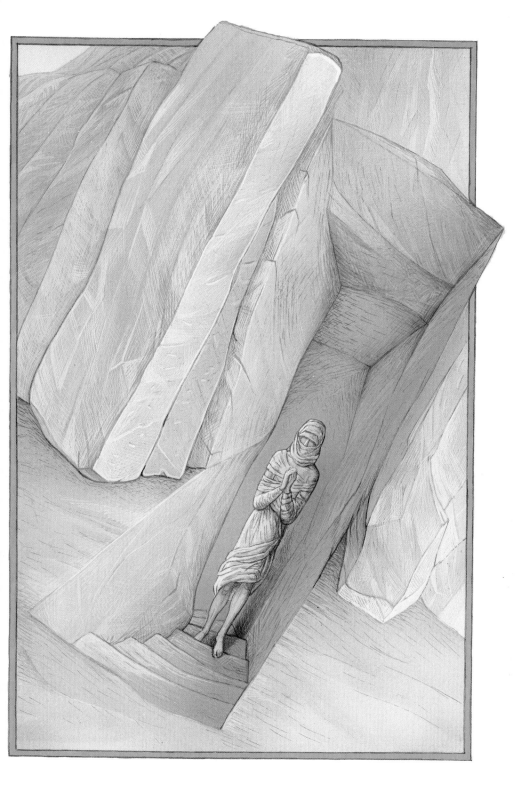

Lazarus' hands and feet were wrapped
with strips of linen.

He had a cloth around his face.

"Unwrap him and let him go,"
said Jesus.

Lazarus was alive!

He wasn't sick anymore.

Then many people believed

that Jesus was God's son.